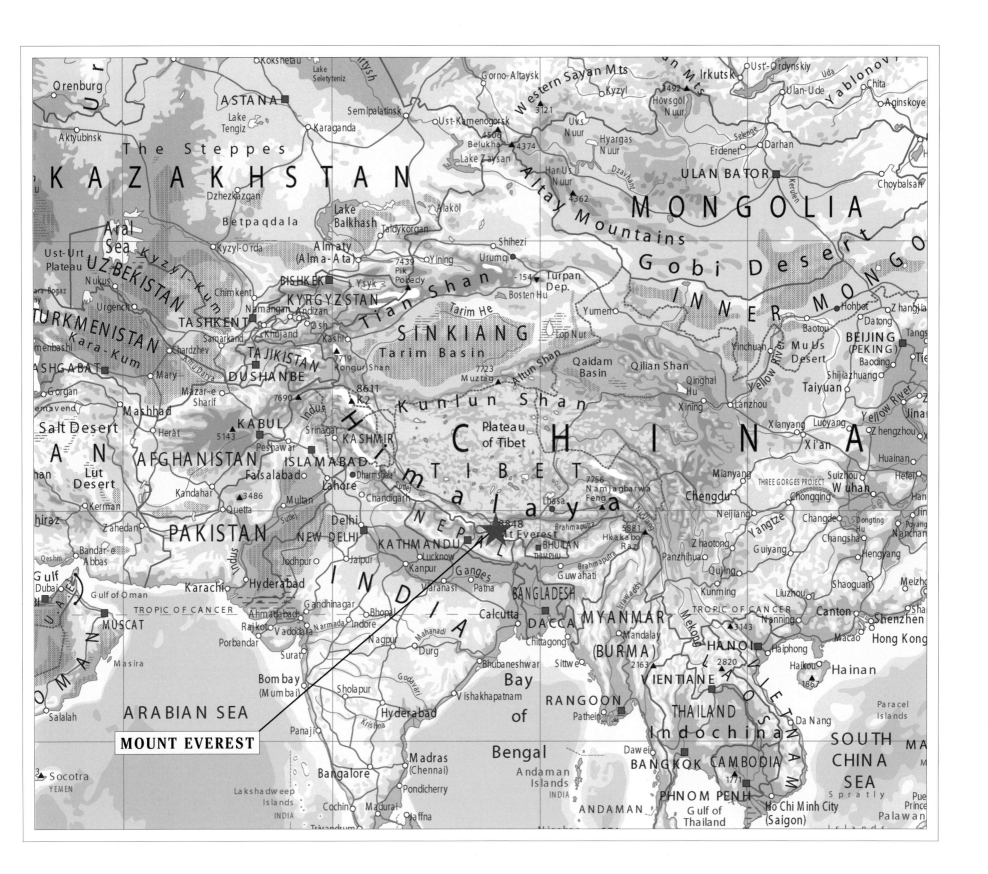

MOUNT EVEREST

Published by Creative Education
123 South Broad Street
Mankato, Minnesota 56001

Creative Education is an imprint of The Creative Company.

Designed by Stephanie Blumenthal
Production design by The Design Lab

Photographs by Corbis (Bettmann, Tom Brakefield, John Van Hasselt, Robert Holmes, Hulton-Deutsch
Collection, Didrik Johnck, David Keaton, Christine Kolisch, Teru Kuwayama, Lake County Museum,
David Lees, Joe McDonald, Warren Morgan, Digital image © 1996 CORBIS; original image courtesy of NASA,
Douglas Peebles, Annie Poole; Papilio, Reuters, Galen Rowell, Royalty-Free, Swim Ink), Geoatlas/World
Vector 3 Map CD, Jake Norton/MountainWorld Photography

Printed in the United States of America

Library of Congress Cataloging-in-Publication Data

Kalz, Jill.
Mount Everest / by Jill Kalz.
p. cm. — (Natural wonders of the world)
ISBN 1-58341-325-1
1. Everest, Mount (China and Nepal)—Juvenile literature. I. Title. II. Series.

DS495.8.E9K35 2004   915.496—dc22   2003065232

First edition

2 4 6 8 9 7 5 3 1

MOUNT EVEREST

JILL KALZ

CREATIVE EDUCATION

FROM BENEATH THE SEA

An imposing pyramid of rock, Mount Everest commands the surrounding Himalayan landscape with its steep slopes and snow-covered peak, visible at the center of this photo (opposite) taken from space by the space shuttle Atlantis.

Snow covers the highest peak on Earth year-round. Nothing grows there. No animals breathe in the thin air save an occasional flock of migrating bar-headed geese or a team of human mountaineers. Its only neighbors are the lesser mountains of the Himalayas below and the **jet stream** whistling above. With its sheer walls of rock and intoxicating elevation, Mount Everest has inspired poets and holy men, scientists and adventurers to "touch the sky" for thousands of years.

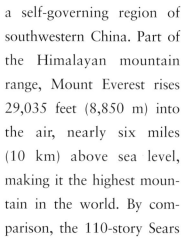

Mount Everest (pronounced EV-er-ist or EV-rist) is a massive, ice-covered pyramid of rock with three distinct sides, or "faces"—the North Face, the Southwest Face, and the East, or Kangshung, Face. The long "seams" that

separate one face from another are the mountain's three major ridges. Everest is located in Asia on the border between Nepal and Tibet, a self-governing region of southwestern China. Part of the Himalayan mountain range, Mount Everest rises 29,035 feet (8,850 m) into the air, nearly six miles (10 km) above sea level, making it the highest mountain in the world. By comparison, the 110-story Sears Tower in Chicago, the tallest building in North America, measures 1,450 feet (440 m). It would take 20 Sears Towers standing end to end to match the height of Mount Everest.

Geologists estimate that the Himalayas are about 50 million years old. Their formation is attributed to the theory of plate tectonics.

Until 1999, when the National Geographic Society measured it using satellite technology and found it to be seven feet (2 m) higher, the height of Everest was listed as 29,028 feet (8,848 m). This measurement was calculated in 1955 through the use of theodolites, surveying instruments that measure both vertical and horizontal angles.

Despite the fact that the Tibetans and Nepalese already had local names for the mountain, the first British explorers to the region named Mount Everest "Peak XV." In 1865, they renamed it "Mount Everest," in honor of Sir George Everest, the Surveyor General of India from 1830 to 1843.

The molten rock responsible for plate movement sometimes breaks through Earth's surface. When it does, it's called lava.

According to this theory, the earth's **crust** is divided into a number of large and small "plates." These plates rest upon a layer of molten rock, called the mantle, just beneath the earth's surface. Instead of remaining in one fixed spot, the plates slide slowly toward or away from each other at rates of up to eight inches (20 cm) per year. Plates are driven by intensely hot gases and liquids escaping from deep within the earth. In areas where plates move against each other, strong geologic activity occurs, such as earthquakes or the formation of volcanoes or mountain ranges.

Long ago, the land masses of India and Asia sat on different plates, separated by an ancient sea called Tethys. Over millions of years, the Indian Plate pushed slowly northward toward Asia, squeezing out the intervening sea in the process. When the Indian Plate collided with the southwestern part of the Eurasian Plate, it pushed rock up from the ocean depths and crumpled the land into the slopes of the Himalayan mountain range. According to some scientists, the Indian Plate is still moving northward, pushing the peaks of the Himalayas, including Mount Everest, higher by as much as a quarter of an inch (5 mm) per year. Were it not for the natural forces of **erosion**, this measurement might be even higher.

6

Mount Everest's closest competition in terms of height is also part of the Himalayas. K2 measures 28,250 feet (8,610 m) tall and is considered by many climbers to be the most dangerous mountain in the world. An Italian expedition made the first successful ascent of K2 in 1954.

Even though many climbers consider K2 a much more challenging climb, conquering the ice-covered slopes of Everest is still a prestigious feat.

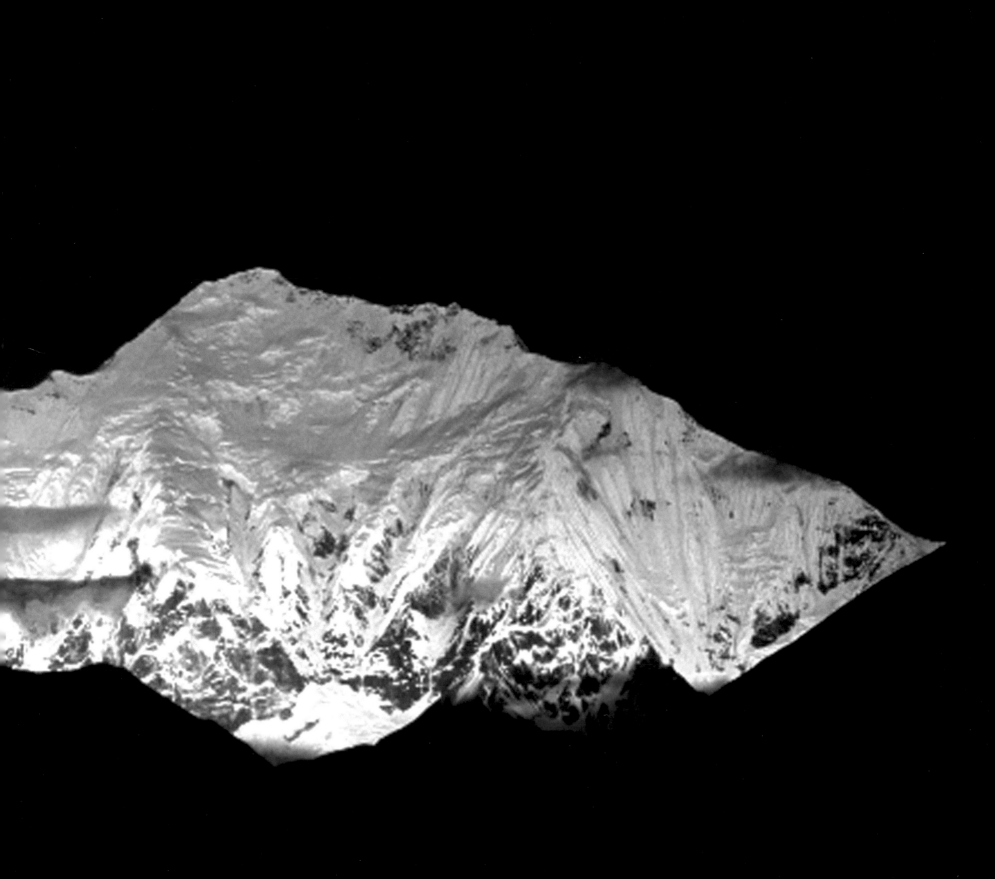

SNAPSHOT OF THE SLOPES

Each spring, flocks of bar-headed geese migrate through the Himalayas—sometimes directly over Everest's peak—to nesting grounds in Tibet. Specially adapted to the extremely cold, oxygen-poor conditions, these geese are the world's highest-altitude migrants and are capable of flying 1,000 miles (1,610 km) in one day with the help of tailwinds.

Because Mount Everest rose from the sea, its peak is capped with dark-gray limestone, a **sedimentary** rock found on the ocean floor. A 500-foot-wide (150 m) belt of yellow limestone, known as the Yellow Band, wraps around the mountain at a height of approximately 27,500 feet (8,380 m). Below this lies a layer of hardened clay called shale, ribboned with bands of extremely hard rock such as  granite and quartzite. Because shale erodes easily, jagged cliffs and **pinnacles** are common on this part of the mountain.

From 24,500 feet (7,470 m) down, Everest consists of gneiss (pronounced NICE), a hard, coarse-grained rock that looks like granite. When the Indian and Eurasian Plates collided, they generated intense pressure and heat which fused together layers of minerals such as feldspar, quartz, and mica, creating the gneiss. This thick band of rock is a remnant of the original tectonic plates.

In January, temperatures on the peak often dip to -33 °F (-36 °C), sometimes plummeting as low as -76 °F (-60 °C). During the summer months, from June to September, temperatures on the peak rise to an average of -2 °F (-19 °C). Summer also marks the start of the **monsoon** season. Most of Mount Everest's annual precipitation falls at this time in the form of snow.

Today's Mount Everest is the product of roughly 50 million years' worth of tectonic plate movements and erosion. Even though the thick layers of gneiss (bottom left) that make up a large portion of the mountain are extremely hard, Everest's rocky slopes are continually worn down and reshaped by wind, precipitation, and massive, slow-moving sheets of ice called glaciers (bottom right).

The people of the Himalayas rely heavily on domesticated herds of yaks for survival. Comfortable at high altitudes, these buffalo-like beasts carry riders and goods up mountain slopes, provide lean meat and rich milk for butter and cheese, and keep people warm with their dense coats and thick hides.

Because of these inhospitable conditions, few signs of life are found on Everest above 18,000 feet (5,485 m). Lower elevations, however, are much warmer and teem with vegetation and wildlife. Forests of pine and hemlock on the lower slopes gradually give way upward to forests of fir and juniper trees mixed with clusters of dwarf birch shrubs. Rhododendron trees bloom pink, white, and purple during the spring and monsoon seasons.

The natural line above or beyond which trees will not grow is called the tree line. On Mount Everest, the tree line starts at about 13,000 feet (4,000 m). Above this line, conditions are too dry and cold to support large vegetation. Ground-hugging herbs and shrubs carpet the slopes at this elevation, gradually thinning to sparse clumps of lichens, mosses, and dwarf grasses. A permanently fixed snow line exists just below 19,000 feet (5,800 m). Nothing grows from this line to the peak.

Plant-eaters such as the musk deer and the goat-like Himalayan tahr prefer feeding on the leaves and grasses of the lower forests and shrub lands. The tahrs' primary natural enemy is the snow leopard. Listed as "endangered," fewer than 7,000 of these cats are thought to roam the mountains of Central Asia today. With heavy, white coats and snowshoe-like paws, snow leopards are well adapted to the cold air of higher elevations. They may climb up to 18,000 feet (5,485 m) to hunt for large prey such as mountain sheep, rodents such as pikas or shrews, or birds such as blood pheasants or snow cocks.

A variety of trees, shrubs, and wildflowers color Everest's lower slopes during the spring and monsoon seasons. Purple poppies (top left) are one of the few blooming plants that can be found at elevations of nearly 19,000 feet (5,800 m).

Special adaptations allow animals on the slopes of Everest to cope with the mountain's rugged, uneven terrain and cold climate. Himalayan tahrs (above), for example, have short, sturdy legs and are covered in a dense, wooly coat. Thick fur also insulates the pika (right), and its small size allows it to find shelter in virtually any crevice.

The elusive snow leopard (left) is at the top of the food chain on the slopes of Mount Everest. Even though it is capable of taking down prey three times its own weight, the cat feeds most often on smaller animals, including pikas, hares, and game birds such as blood pheasants (right).

BECAUSE IT IS THERE

British mountaineers (opposite) made the very first attempts at an Everest summit in the early 1920s. Local peoples had had no interest in reaching the peak, as the mountain was considered sacred, but they marked places of religious significance on the slopes with mani stone mounds (below), rocks inscribed with Buddhist mantras or images.

Until 1953, no human had ever stood atop the peak of Mount Everest. In fact, since neither Nepal nor Tibet welcomed outsiders before the turn of the 20th century, no Westerner had even come within 60 miles (100 km) of Mount Everest's foothills until 1913. Cloaked in snow and ice, the mountain was considered sacred by local people. Tibetans called the soaring peak *Chomolungma*, "Goddess Mother of the World." The Nepalese called it *Sagarmatha*, "Forehead of the Sky."

In 1921, a British **reconnaissance** team finally received permission from Tibet to explore Everest's North and East Faces. The team failed to summit (reach the peak) that year and the next, but one team member, George Leigh Mallory, decided to make a third attempt in 1924. When asked why he wanted to climb Mount Everest, Mallory replied, "Because it is there."

On the morning of June 8, 1924, Mallory and partner Andrew Irvine set out for the summit from their **camp** at 26,700 feet (8,138 m). Hours later, clouds shrouded the peak, and

1 6

News of the Hillary-Tenzing conquest of Everest reached London on June 2, 1953, the same day Britain's new queen, Elizabeth II, was crowned. The news was so big that the *Times*, London's largest newspaper, printed a photo of the mountain, not the queen, at the top center of its front page.

Mallory and Irvine disappeared. No one ever saw them alive again. Seventy-five years later, Mallory's frozen body was discovered on Mount Everest's North Face. Irvine's body is still missing. To this day, the debate continues as to whether Mallory and Irvine died on their way up to the summit, or on their way down.

Other expeditions tried—unsuccessfully—to summit Everest in the 1930s and 1940s. In 1950, China invaded Tibet and closed all northern approaches to the mountain, keeping them closed until 1979. Luckily, Nepal simultaneously opened its doors, allowing foreigners to attempt Everest from the south for the first time. New Zealand beekeeper Edmund Hillary, an experienced mountaineer, rose to the challenge. As part of a British expedition, Hillary and native Nepalese climber Tenzing Norgay Sherpa finally conquered Mount Everest on the morning of May 29, 1953.

Tenzing Norgay Sherpa and Edmund Hillary (opposite), part of a British-led expedition to Everest in 1953, were the first two people to reach the highest point on Earth. Soon after the conquest, expedition members were welcomed in Great Britain as national heroes (left).

As of 2003, the oldest person to conquer Everest was 70, the youngest 15. The first American was Jim Whittaker (1963). Japan's Junko Tabei was the first woman (1975). One of the first climbers to ascend without oxygen bottles was Italian Reinhold Messner, who was also the first to solo (1980).

Since the 1953 summit, more than 1,200 people have reached Mount Everest's peak via 15 different routes—some in groups, some alone, with and without supplemental oxygen—and more than 175 climbers have died. Avalanches, hurricane-force winds, and **hypothermia** are dangers from which no expedition is immune. The Khumbu icefall, a shifting glacier at the base of the mountain, has claimed a number of lives in its deep crevasses and is considered one of the most dangerous parts of a southern ascent. Also, climbers in the air above 26,000 feet (7,925 m)—a region called the "Death Zone"—breathe in just one-third of the oxygen available at sea level. It's like "running on a treadmill and breathing through a straw," according to one respected climber. Prolonged exposure to oxygen-poor air can lead to a potentially fatal condition called **edema**. But despite the emotional and physical toll Everest can take on a climber, hundreds continue to flock to the slopes each year for a chance to stand atop the world.

Despite the latest advances in gear, attempting to reach Everest's peak is still a dangerous, humbling endeavor for any climber. Mountaineers must risk extreme cold, deadly falls, and a lack of oxygen to make the ascent.

OPEN FOR BUSINESS

All climbers feel the effects of high-altitude sickness to some degree. Lower oxygen levels in the blood lead to headaches, nausea, fitful sleep, and pronounced fatigue. Without bottled oxygen, the body actually starts to die within the "Death Zone," and climbers may hallucinate, hearing orchestras and seeing ghosts.

Originally from eastern Tibet, the Sherpas are an ethnic group of **Buddhists** who immigrated to Nepal in the early 1500s. Those who settled in the Khumbu region beneath Mount Everest have lent their compassionate spirit and physical stamina to nearly every climbing expedition since the 1920s.

Although Sherpas traditionally made their living by growing potatoes and herding yaks, today more than 75 percent of those in the Khumbu region are involved in the tourist trade. They work as **porters**, guides, and hotel and restaurant owners. Schools, hospitals, water systems, and airstrips have been built, thanks in large part to tourist dollars and Edmund Hillary, who since his famous summit has made it his life's mission to improve the lives of the Sherpas.

But tourism has a dark side, too. More tourists mean more trash. Discarded cans, tents, ropes, oxygen bottles, and human waste litter Everest's slopes. Also, for many years, the Nepalese harvested large areas of forest and shrubs as fuel wood for the mountaineers, which destroyed animal habitats and left the soil vulnerable to erosion. In addition, many veteran climbers worry that too many climbing permits are being issued—diminishing Everest's mystique—and to too many inexperienced climbers, which can lead to deadly bottlenecks on the mountain's narrow paths. Some veterans also bemoan the fact that

22

No one knows Everest more intimately than the Sherpas of the Khumbu region. Record holders include Babu Chiri Sherpa (opposite bottom) and Appa Sherpa (opposite top, with his family), who has ascended a record 14 times. Strings of prayer flags (top) and stone chortens (bottom) on the mountain slopes, testaments to the lives of fallen Sherpas, illustrate the Sherpas' strong Buddhist faith.

Today's climbing gear makes use of the most durable, lightweight materials available. Crampons, metal spikes that attach to climbing boots, in combination with an ice axe, help climbers gain sure footing on the icy slopes.

Everest is now "tied down" with thousands of feet of fixed ropes and rigged with scores of aluminum ladders to make the ascent easier.

Thankfully, the Nepalese government has been trying to clean up the mountain in recent years. It now requires climbers to bring down their own trash and gear or forfeit a $4,000 deposit. In an effort to help preserve the native vegetation and wildlife to the south and west of Everest, the Sagarmatha National Park was established in 1976. China's Qomolangma National Nature Preserve lies to the north and east. Cutting wood is now prohibited around the mountain, and climbers must bring their own fuel. Reforestation projects have become a priority.

Pleas to reduce the number of permits

issued each year, however, have so far gone unheeded. It is a difficult decision: give Everest a rest, and the thousands of people in the area whose lives depend solely upon the tourists and their money will suffer; do nothing, and the world's tallest mountain becomes mired in **commercialism**.

Fifty million years ago, rock from deep beneath Earth's surface was forced up into the thin air, pushed into the clouds until it towered above all else on the planet. The home of the gods, the burial ground of the unlucky, or the ultimate mountaineering prize, Mount Everest has enchanted people for centuries. No other mountain has made us feel so big and grand, and so small and insignificant, all at the same time.

2 4

Despite the permanently fixed ropes and ladders designed to make an ascent of Everest easier, conquering the mountain still requires great skill. Smart climbers will begin training at least one year before the actual climb. Activities such as biking, swimming, playing tennis, sprinting, rowing, and weight lifting all help prepare climbers for the demands of Everest.

SEEING THE WONDER

In 1996, a film crew climbed to the top of the world to shoot *Everest*, the first large-format (IMAX) documentary of the mountain. Ninety yaks and 40 porters carried three tons (2.7 t) of food, film, and gear, including a 42-pound (19 kg) camera, for the two-month venture.

The most popular tourist route to Everest is through Kathmandu (right) and the village of Namche Bazaar (opposite).

Most people don't have the money or skill to attempt Everest itself, but a visit to Nepal's Khumbu region, which sprawls to the south and west of the mountain, can be just as rewarding.

October and November are the most popular months for tourists. The countryside is lush and green, the weather warm, and visibility excellent. Fly into Kathmandu, Nepal's capital, then take one of the daily flights to Lukla, a village just south of Sagarmatha National Park. There are no paved roads within the 425 square miles (1,105 sq km) of the Khumbu valley—no cars, buses, or bikes—so pack light! You will have to walk a lot, across all kinds of terrain, so you shouldn't visit unless you're in excellent health. Getting used to the higher elevation will take some time.

At 11,300 feet (3,440 m), the village of Namche Bazaar is the visitor gateway to the region. Sightseeing treks offer breathtaking views of Everest and neighboring peaks. While Nepali is the official language, most locals understand English.

Mountaineers usually train for more than a year to prepare for the two and a half

Sherpas are phenomenal high-altitude climbers. In 2004, Pemba Dorjee Sherpa broke the record for the fastest ascent from Base Camp to the Everest summit in just over eight hours (most climbers take four days). That same year, Appa Sherpa summited for the 14th time, more than any other person.

month (on average) trek from the foothills to Everest's summit. Their first stop is **Base Camp**. From there, climbers make numerous trips up and down the mountain, hauling supplies to ever higher camps. Typical expeditions make four camps beyond Base Camp. Staggering the climb instead of starting at the bottom and heading straight up helps climbers gradually adjust to the thin air.

Attempting Everest is costly. The Nepalese government charges $70,000 for a seven-person team. China charges $5,000 for 10 or fewer. Climbers pay additional tens of thousands of dollars for various access permits, transportation, support staff (guides, porters, cooks), food, camping and climbing gear, and even special Buddhist rituals to bless the expedition.

Before traveling to Nepal, check for travel safety warnings. In 1996, a civil war broke out that has since claimed the lives of 7,000 people. A cease-fire was declared in January 2003. Even though Sherpas say Khumbu visitors have nothing to fear (no tourists have been killed), curfews are still in place, and armed soldiers patrol villages and park trails.

Tenzing Norgay Sherpa once said that of all the things necessary for a successful climb, cheerfulness and teamwork are the most important.

M O U N T  E V E R E S T

QUICK FACTS

Elevation: 29,035 feet (8,850 m), an altitude commonly used by cruising passenger jets

Location: On the border between Nepal and Tibet, within Asia's Himalayan mountain range

Age: ~ 50 million years

Composition: Dark rock, mostly gneiss, with hardened shale and sandstone, granite, and limestone

Average summer temperature (summit): -2 °F (-19 °C)

Average winter temperature (summit): -33 °F (-36 °C)

First person to summit: New Zealander Edmund Hillary, with Tenzing Norgay Sherpa, on May 29, 1953, via the South route; Hillary was knighted by Britain's Queen Elizabeth in 1953 for his achievement

First woman to summit: Junko Tabei, from Japan, on May 16, 1975, via the Southeast Ridge route

Climbing season: Generally March 1 to May 31, before the onset of the monsoons

Number of people who have reached the summit (2003 data): More than 1,200 people from 63 countries; 89 reached the summit on one day in 2001

Number of people who have died on the mountain (2003 data): 175

Deadliest climbing season: 1996, when a record 15 climbers perished, 8 in one storm; the tragedy is recounted in the bestselling book *Into Thin Air,* by Jon Krakauer

Wildlife: Mammals such as musk deer, Himalayan tahrs, snow leopards, yaks, and a variety of rodents, including pikas, shrews, and moles; birds such as blood pheasants, snow cocks, and crow-like birds called choughs

Other names: *Sagarmatha* (Nepal); *Chomolungma* (Tibet)

Base Camp—a "tent city" base of operations for climbers preparing to summit, located at 17,550 feet (5,350 m) on the Khumbu glacier

Buddhists—followers of Buddhism, a peaceful religion founded in India in the sixth century B.C. by the Buddha, a religious teacher

camp—tents set up on the mountainside to give climbers an opportunity to rest and adjust to the thin air

commercialism—the practice of buying and selling goods with an unhealthy emphasis on profit, often at the expense of people, animals, or the environment

crust—the solid, outermost layer of the earth; the mantle and the core lie beneath

edema—a potentially fatal condition in which excess fluid collects in a person's brain or lungs

erosion—the wearing away by wind, water, or chemicals; when soil erodes, its nutrients are carried away and plants cannot grow

geologists—scientists who specialize in geology, the study of the earth's history and composition, including its crust, interior, and types of rocks

hypothermia—a potentially fatal condition in which a person's body loses heat faster than it can produce it, dropping body temperature to subnormal levels

jet stream—bands of high-velocity winds that circle the earth from west to east at an altitude of 8 to 10 miles (13–16 km)

monsoon—a seasonal wind of the Indian Ocean and southern Asia that delivers torrential rains

pinnacles—pointed formations that resemble church spires; the top of a mountain, its peak, is a pinnacle

porters—people who are hired to carry goods; Everest porters (usually Sherpas) carry loads on their backs, anchored with wide straps across their foreheads

reconnaissance—a detailed, information-gathering study; the 1921 reconnaissance team searched the slopes of Everest for a possible route to the summit

sedimentary—formed by the settling of sediment, or matter, carried by wind or water; sand at the bottom of a river, for example, is sediment

INDEX

climate 10, 30

climbers, famous
   Hillary, Edmund 18, 22, 40
   Irvine, Andrew 16, 18
   Mallory, George Leigh 16, 18
   Norgay, Tenzing 18, 30

climbing 16, 18, 20, 24, 28, 30
   costs 28
   dangers 20
   deaths 20, 30
   permits 22, 24
   records 20, 28
   season 30
   training 28

conservation 24

"Death Zone" 20, 22

Elizabeth II (queen of England) 18, 30

Everest (IMAX movie) 26

Into Thin Air (book) 30

K2 7

Khumbu region 22, 26, 28

Mount Everest
   age 4, 30
   composition 10, 30
   faces 4
   first summit (female) 20, 30
   first summit (male) 18, 30
   formation. *See* plate tectonics
   geographical location 4, 30
   height 4, 5, 30
   names, other 6, 16, 30
   ridges 4

Namche Bazaar, Nepal 26

plant life 12

plate tectonics 4, 6, 10

Sherpas 18, 22, 28

tourism 22, 24, 26, 28
   negative effects of 22, 24

wildlife 10, 12, 30